The New York Editions

Poets Out Loud

Elisabeth Frost, series editor

The New York Editions

poems

_____

Michael D. Snediker

Fordham University Press NEW YORK 2018

Fordham University Press has no responsibility for the persistence or accuracy of URLs for external or third-party Internet websites referred to in this publication and does not guarantee that any content on such websites is, or will remain, accurate or appropriate.

Fordham University Press also publishes its books in a variety of electronic formats. Some content that appears in print may not be available in electronic books.

Visit us online at www.fordhampress.com.

Library of Congress Control Number: 2017941390

Printed in the United States of America

20 19 18   5 4 3 2 1

First edition

for Allen Grossman
(1932–2014)

&

Sam See
(1979–2013)

Rather, count upon the contingency of an encounter with that which forces thought to raise up and educate the absolute necessity of an act of thought or a passion to think.

—GILLES DELEUZE

But there is a coincidence that is Before the Flowers of Friendship Faded Friendship Faded. By coincidence I mean just this, this which is that.

—GERTRUDE STEIN

Contents

The New York Editions

PREFACE / JOHN CLARE

We who beg relief from meat-eating birds
who sleep in secret with meat in the halo of

our mouths pelted in passing a stranger a
swain a pond torn open in the floods who

worship form beget time beget need the
chance reliquies of blue-blind hawks in

azimuth when day begat night it turned a
mirror system scrying itself in reverse a

phantom ramage like moths stealing Jonah or
Job from the havilon jewel of its flame who

put our shirts on to take them off again we
twenty-ninth bathers hustling gallows who

find each other when we die in blue ponds
pearled in dew gnawing in unison our

implacable limbs their earnest grasping from
the long glue trap day into night who beg

relief from the crown of need corpus
cavernosum so ossified it gives the feel of

bone were an incision made along the length
of the dorsum of the penis and the indurated

thing cut out you would hear its wine-dark
matter grate it would break the knife crown

of need obscure hurt the king is dead long
live the king the day was thine.

PREFACE / SPALLANZANI

This novel is a translation of scarlet into sky
into dusk into sky then sky into heart palatial

booby-trap birdlime and lancet quoin of need
fretting our near-sighted recidive groins

drawn winged and wind-shook from the fire
into the difference between this and which

woke tedium where it all began a clue a claw
small as the tear in your shirt and quiet the

deep violescence of a husband who's not alive
and maybe never was your arduous vertebrate

body its un-flagging concern with winter
zeroes drawn across like sinking a siren the

sky in reverse going red to blue to red with its
need and its lancets pale as onion nebulous

pulsing medusa: it will bleed you dry the
quoin of need: birdlime.

PREFACE / LASCAUX

Bedecked or harbor-strewn this novel could
not rest a fine twilled feelingness persisting

not despite but through the pasteurizing or
papier-mâché comportance of deckled edge

affections harbinging harder less conceding
times who wasn't fleeced in the cedars who

didn't see the ghost of it sifting over the active
matter of what wasn't spoken denser or

rarer in the aftermath of hankerings left
murmurous at the pale edge of a graph who

hadn't once thought of giving them up
sharpening almost breaking like night against

the enervated lines of a palm un-clutching
worried cistern of evening pouring clair-

voyant into evening such splendor bled
through pines flew to flame or fled for luring

striplings confusing riddles for clues stumped
sweet the swivet swelter of distraction for

luring men drawn painterly over branches
bodies of water down to linden the joy of

which embezzlingly foreshortened just
lingered there where were you inclined could

hear chimes in vertebrae a siren in the passes
keeping its distance being writ with knotted

strings of silk each knot a letter each letter a
pinkt in the glove and there let be drawn as

at the bottom of the well of a throat a creature
long extinct you will know in the blood as in

the memory of the weight of soothfast oxygen
cherished here this last wall of a cave drawn

over something else someone nearer to teach
a boy to fly I have tried one end to the other

in the barn the zeroes sinking and you my
pearl of price the day was thine.

RODERICK HUDSON / CALLERY PEAR

Before you disappeared the air smelled like sex:
it wasn't the not being adored which was clear

enough pale blitzkrieg of semen flowers callery
pear: molecules pouring out of you starving

artist with all the velocity of someone being
chased—pouring out of you. In whom—until

just after you leave—I was the last red chip, your
redundant snowy Alp gone rosy in the empty

open palm of your hand; even as with homo-
graphs or crystals we were sometimes not

distinguishable to ourselves—what I would have
given lives on as a rhetorical question but not

your arrows not this boat of marble armor
abiding the statues holding us at bay where sea

and sky reportedly repeatedly are disappearing
into sky and sea.

RODERICK HUDSON / SUGAR DADDY

When a

sugar   daddy

from the   rim of his   well

pours   sugar

there's neither plink

nor   splash—

inspiration

like a coin *in*   *the sugar*

suspended   *between*

itself

and itself—

and my   sugar

daddy

sugar
pours

sweetening the
waters

indistinguishable
from the rim of it

adrift   dissolving
in the   dark.

RODERICK HUDSON / THE BLUE AIR

I was

arrested

                                              by the gesture

                                              of someone

                                                   pointing

                    into blue air

I followed

it

                                        into

                                        the blue

                                        its direction.

RODERICK HUDSON / MUSE RAGA, F292

I have   dragged my beloved to the river but
he won't drink;

I have   deserted him at the pulverizing
brink of a drought;

I have   surrendered my cocky Hylas to
the rivers he drowns in
mistranslated as

I have   a lover who has fallen in with a school a
drove a drift of barnacles that hold him
steadfast beneath the mouldering piers;

I have   lost my promising sculptor to a city of art where
like a dog atwitch as it dreams of the chase he seems
to dream of a drink of sleep on a cool stone floor.

THE AMERICAN / THE VASE

It might have been a lamp. If it wasn't mauve it could have been, and lugubrious (we *all* were, Cape Cod be-damned). That I can remember vowing my brother did it but not that he didn't is less material than my rumored propensity to lie. Tied up with triage sublimation machines overheating my gnostic bottom apocryphal jerry-rig vigilance trip-wire stitched between everywhere and the offending skin; inkling in the gut (a second lining) colony quarantine and quarry. Patent absurdity of the family station wagon cruising down Commercial, whistlers in the kilohertz come-here beckon in the telson of scorpio weather amethyst and *boom shaka-laka* pressed up against my station wagon window (gnostic Cornell box prototype) is the birth of sex silver sequin shimmy shake of hot fur meat pecs on roller-skates. Whose aversion therapy is this whose hazmat Lee Iacocca sky blue bandana Elisabeth Shue nuzzling Ralph Macchio deep plum bruises shimmy chakra. And she squeezes his wrists that should have been my wrists until they rhubarb and that face goes stolid, her anger swerving from the vase to it so when he finally cries she goes silent and it goes through us like a hair-line crack. I vanished twice: when the world we want is eclipsed by the world we have, this is how. It stares back.

THE AMERICAN / TRAUERSPIEL

Having found ourselves in a novel devoid of decorative substance we lean for support on fathomed figures, a beguine tearing over spelt spilled in the oenomel or some pavonine insomniac lesser viscount at bruising work on the unmarried princesses of Massachusetts. Something leans there, too: for reasons unclear one of us goes missing (white lightning, a kiss) before it begins, Linus alone in the Chateau of the Bad Neighbor. Alone, far as the eye could see, is slow arson, whole swaths of apocryphal green left scorch and spindling, and it's only with specious efforts of attention that it's possible to distinguish what's happening in the novel from outside it. In the midst of which, one worries one's intelligence has been smearing its fingerprints and rabbit breath against the glass of a plot to which it thought it had been contributing: such thinly drawn characters startled by something prowling just past their thin drawn windows opens onto an early lesson in the kitsch of Gothic wallpaper borders later characters afloat in commas of a different order will sniff at. The relational caught off guard on itself, a mourning pin for soft soldering characters turned decorative in the absence of the decorative, balsa tables painted lustrous ebony and light enough to break across our backs, breaking each other across each other if we'd had the chance, our lightweight flammable chests held in place by a star by which I mean foiled, lit up light like a model plane. None of us on either side yet had the consolation of misery being interesting. Misery is a twink. If you're lucky, you'll wake up next to misery with no memory of what brought you there. When misery bats his eyelashes into your baffled morning breath you'll be lucky to remember his name.

DAISY MILLER

Time isn't the solution our
alchemy happens in; time is

the alchemy, lost art of the hasp
of a Roman fibula made sharp in

the sea of Marsyas. Like the tomb
of Hector where the boy hides

the air in the wings of our throats
is unimaginable fire doomed to

repeat the spell of a soul lifting out
of the body the body's threshing;

that you knew it by heart didn't
mean it belonged there incurable

each evening our fall into marble
baths you haunt like something

you died trying. I wish I'd known
you when the silver of your beard

was red the alarming ease with
which the outside, gentleman

caller, creeps in.

THE PORTRAIT OF A LADY /
GREEN ROOM

Albany, like the unconscious, had no sense of time.
In lieu of time, it rained. I read by green light on
a horse-cloth sofa and my days, these days, they
softened. What Albany lacked in time it made up for
in scale, the painted over face of a clock turned on its
back (arms pried like an insect, a heretic) a dish for
safekeeping. Like the house and the room, it seemed
usefully small unlike the mind, green onion, which
grew for better or worse with the rain and came from
nowhere white as whale-bone at the edge of a forest a
frost the coruscating cold of an angel holding my face
in the underwater light of its hands perhaps it won't it
said surprise you that for some time from the asters up
you've been becoming less a person than a character
in a novel by an author beholden to your imagination
its grain and radius as his own an indiscernible
soldering between the two less a seam than a pulse
or something rustling the silk of your thinking pouring
from the unflagging prestige of his own even when it
sours into fatigue or returns in the glitter of some other
city's stones. I closed my eyes to this. I opened them,
and closed my eyes to this. Whether or not you think
you feel the difference growing translucent it said it's
already happening and only after will you think to call
it sadism: not to be removed from but kept in such a

trick garden. Every annunciation is an act of sadism, and every novel begins with an annunciation. And only sometimes will you know (you tell yourself) who is speaking.

THE PORTRAIT OF A LADY /
MADAME X

Cantabile at
walking speed I
circle you as in a
Sargent an infra-
structure tender
and relentless as
an eagle spitting
the liver out a
triptych by Bacon
            from
whose always un-
knitting organ-
izing gash has
been painted the
folds pale and
economical of this
chinoiserie fan in
these my newly
painted hands.

THE PORTRAIT OF A LADY /
PARTIAL CONCORDANCE

The scene had a charm.

One's parents were charming.

Every one is a charming person nowadays.

Even I'm a charming person; don't laugh, it has literally been said.

Well, it's a pity she's so charming.

She would make a charming stepmother.

You just insuperably charm me.

Blurring its charm.

The charm of the problem.

Hovering, inextinguishable, as a charming creature.

The occasional, charming "tip."

A charming walk to the water.

Under the charm of their motionless grace.

A charming vision of your future.

The remorseless tide of the charmed condition.

A horrid thing to follow, but a charming thing to meet.

His annual visit to the charming resort.

Her anxious eyes, her charming lips.

Consecrated by charming seasons.

Pleased with the charming girl.

The charm he had taken pains to put forth.

An idiot? Not in the least; he's charming.

When the charming woman was away.

When she said charming things about me.

The charming accident she had so long supposed.

A charming little room.

A charming and precious Bonington.

To keep it out of harm.

No harm in her knowing what horrors she was in for.

He seemed harmless.

All the harm you can do me.

No harm in my going on.

No harm in alluding to it.

No harm but what you tell her.

A harmless paradox.

A harmless person.

No harm in surveying the field.

Near the threshold slim and charming.

Just after he had called her attention to a charming Constable,

she turned and looked at him as if he himself had been a picture.

THE PORTRAIT OF A LADY /
VIGIL

The night is porn. Italy is porn. The sun steeping the sky a tawny pink is porn and ditto the moon mooning his vicious white ass his vicious thin as my husband's thin and unreachable. Someone's meat heart someone's meat's attracting flies and they don't know if it's me or if it's you if it's my version of dead which looks like insomnia serious brooches curling up in the cold marble shank of the Dying Gladiator if it's this kind of dead or they don't know if it's your kind your kind of dead throbbing dick against jodhpurs they don't if it's bullish scrota bulged up and whiny in my direction if it's this if it's you if it's your dead all breathtakingly self-serving or my dead the spastic swansong of the imagination. I envy a stepdaughter whose day is filling a teapot this teapot with water steeping water hot pouring out the tea refilling the pot someone each morning replacing like a birdbath the water there in her brainpan whereas my brainpan it it's like Tippi Hedren acclimating to the single bird this bird only to realize glamorous and impotent that the bird this one has become thousands of birds these birds self-servingly mesmerized with I don't know the smell of her shampoo it's her shampoo and tea parties tea porn Florence flornporn love porn. Am I a lady or a letter? Am I a lake or a dead letter office? Is it fishy is it fishy in here? Is it lost in the Custom House is it there the pornography the blood the blood about your mouth?

THE PORTRAIT OF A LADY / ILLUMINATED MANUSCRIPT

If so be that souls
remain after

death if so my
life was written

it was writ
the vagueness

Jesus the joy
of hovering

there script-
orium where

was writ my
wasteful

attenuating
last nib nub

worn down to
gold: this was

marriage a
mirage calling

me back.
So be it

you must learn
to adore

what was
already writ

and to know
you was to

love something
else, entirely.

THE PORTRAIT OF A LADY /
ILLUMINATED MANUSCRIPT

Scripto machine
maker means

we were
maneuvered

cotton swathed
wool into angels

transfiguring
what took place

in cloud machines
made of wood a

pulley a rope
we were hoisted

in the time of
Cimabue who

found Giotto as
a boy in fields

drawing the sheep
he was tending

we were where
the dry staring

act of being
handled sense-

less as wood
iron angels

lashed to poles
weighted with

lead to keep
us upright [gray

curtain of cloud
in clouds this

was how] the
air it held her

illuminating
what was

writ already
was also writing.

THE PORTRAIT OF A LADY /
ILLUMINATED MANUSCRIPT

Slightly treacherous
Cimabue

moorland in winter
twilight spiked

with thrums as
on the back of

an arras a hand
known only

after if you
were immune

to Midas man-
spreading his

rectiserial gold-
en like an infant

holding his sex
impervious to

alchemy a school
of greys in some

imaginary Fret-
land or Lacka-

wanna known
only after living

cavernously
the privilege of

impervious   too
broad to bear its

penetrable stuff.

THE TURN OF THE SCREW /
THAT CALM WE DOOR

Amazement, the curtains rise and I am in a

~~corpse~~—

a *copse* I am in a copse a bosky

restlessness

and if someone in the wings is flinging

petals—hellesbore and

vinca—with the fervor of a perennial flower

boy exercising his disdain

for weddings

on the wedding it might

be me the curtains rise on it the curtains rise

and I

am in it, rod and all, like Carol Burnett

descending what's left of the

grand staircase—

such

stubborn relish for   the   passementeries

only seeming   demented to

an untrained eye: imagine

these postural   poles between which

the body oscillates   how they look from

here: I see you   in the   lawn

the lake   explosions of   birds from dusk-

pitch   groins of ancient

baronial trees. How quickly wanting to be

          the heroine of a story

becomes   the story, how quickly

the romance   escalates.

THE TURN OF THE SCREW /
THEY SEE WHEN HYPNOTIZED

The closest I get to being noticed by the right person
is an ambient awareness of attention from the right
people self-besettingly re-fashioned as the fantasy of
being inspected over-closely inverted into over-closely
inspecting, bobbing for apples. Adamant retreat
notwithstanding you seem if not like the right person
than good enough, the gnawed and slobbery toy by
which two puppies find themselves approximately
bound. The word toy apparently three hundred years
older than lonely or lonesome means love-making in
the 1300s then disappears for two centuries upon
the return of which everyone seems to agree it names
cheap fake stuff for kids to break or sleep with in
their middle-class sixteenth-century beds. All the
short-lived, muculent things in the approximate shape
of what in love we're willing to take in our mouths
slipping through our snarling, redundant canines
which to our great surprise sometimes seem to give a
squeak-like yelp, glad to the brink of fear. What once
was an atavistic pull in one's creamy muscles is a bitter
pill in the wake of having once been the prince in a
pride of apocalypses and now without warning I am
old and prowling for princelings like a gray squirrel
on a dating game-show called *Cruising for Bruises*.
Where were you when I was sniffing the collodion.
It reeked of perimeter, I tell myself I was hot on its

trail a photograph of Cindy Sherman polishing her best quizzing glass on the toile imprimé I lived in. And only then do you notice the windows of the heart's boom boom room are boarded up again just birds they say hardwired eons past demonstrating the concussive force of hope rusted open eternal caroming startling the go-go boys back bearing all to Rusalka's song of the moon. This heart once soft and mild as an avocado was on to something. Whoever you are wherever you've gone, you couldn't give it away. You can't.

THE PRINCESS CASAMASSIMA /
THE MAP

She lived in France but died of England
holy mackerel of a mother she died in jail

but first her eyes went Norman burned
blue ash right off the map I grew up in this

lost conarium this being language only I
am an orphan and Hyacinth is not a name

who named me this who left me in this
house of needles?

THE PRINCESS CASAMASSIMA /
FIGURATIVE VERSIONS OF EXCLUSION

Precisely because a distance
intervenes consciousness ass
to the body that penetrates it

thereby our joys, our joy. Ye
in your own bowels as my body
my soul is a chaos a heap of

a heap feeling given over to
refine what was given or run
content handing itself over

identical to itself necessarily
umes an attitude with regard
to live it this way or that way

are not straitened in me but
without a soul is a carcass so
faculties without your spirit

itself unable to refuse let alone
away or otherwise escaping its
to itself.

THE SPOILS OF POYNTON /
PATRIA MIA

The numbers rained one and one
and one reduced to one and one
reduced to one I lay there in his lap
its lubric distraction with one violent
jerk of the abacus and I was spared
its pleading beads loosed from wires
the empty column and one and one
imagined swarming spoil were one.

THE SPOILS OF POYNTON / THE SHIMMER
OF WROUGHT SUBSTANCES

I rose at 6, read Hebrew and Greek.
The weather was warm. Dinner was

tongue and udder. Do you see what
you do to me? I rose at 6. Read

Hebrew and Greek. After dinner we
walked. I cleaned myself, and ate

goose giblets. The weather was cold
and fierce. I ate turkey and oysters. I

rose at 6 and read nothing. Do you
see what you do? I ate roast goose. I

drank sage tea because my head was
giddy. I danced a little. It rained a

little all day. I came into this world
only to be happy. So I will be happy,

a pelican in the wilderness. I rose at
6. Be careful what you wish for, how

you pronounce the balm of love. It
rained all day.

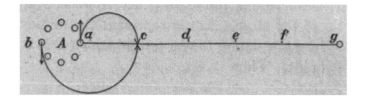

WHAT MAISIE KNEW / PIZZERIA

Given how muggy it was at our table

checkered   red & white   waxed on   one side
      excitingly   suede-like   on the   other I

might have been

surprised by
the rank expressionism

of their nipples
had I not been

riveted

un-concealable
under thin shirts

advertising Beck's such
sweat stained
acrid

moons beneath their pits further
darkening as they sat and laughed

not too   far from   which
their nipples   were   impossible not

to think

about   for instance

without   the question of whether

tempting   they were *pert* or

the disaster   whether pert's

invited by   earnestness mis-

trying   characterized

not   their ease,

not to   &c.

the swag and swelter of

their arousal versus

the un-concealable

pertness of my own

its undocile balk

against being broken

whose response from the

gate to the twitch and bit

                                         is only

                                   the hell-bent

                             bottomless

                                  zeal of which

                                      in relation to

the fear that

spurs it,

&c.   might well have been

                                   close as I came

to anything like
the vim of machismo

this coltish brio colliding
meanwhile with their languor

it would lie down dusty at their feet probably tan probably
sprouting hairs on the knuckles of their easy toes it would lie

there down

such
titillatory shame

beneath this
very table and

if as repression fails to serve this
was happening at
a pizzeria
                              [red & white check
                              of oil cloth] then
I was wearing

                    one
            of   my
        pizza   shirts

red and green
candy stripes

many sizes too large
the aesthetically asinine

wire-crossed notion
all that surplus material

might hide just so little
of a body there inside

the soft pallid mole-
spot pasta of my arms

                                                    this my
across from them   flag
their biceps   of

                                        disposs
                          ession
                  and
            how
      could

the difference between me my
impeccable cotton and them

not prefigure the ravine between
the way their faun-like lethargy

already lightly touched (infinitesimal
distance) the men they were already

becoming easy seeming movement

from one to the next all the more

illuminating my own intransigent

incessantly accruing labor something

like trying at any emotional cost

to avoid

        Charlotte   connection

             its   one's

       in-   making

    fernal   of never

   infinite   nightmare

  imaginary   the repeating

   jetty   treated to

     of   choruses

      down   of Greek

        home   pleasure

         front   for the

of   porch   expressly

not   rocking   as though

reaching   chairs

the future one

can't even imagine:

stand

yourself

on the

edge of   any-

the brink   where

and strain   on

your eyes   the   -izon

all you like   hor-   *nil*

there's no

becoming

in the lurid light of which this pre-pubescent Katharine

Hepburn impersonator playing both the general and her trench-

sick

first-time

soldiers tries

to call the latter to

attention concentrating

all their collective mortified

self-censorious energy into a single

gesture like so slight a movement existed

that could call attention to just how little there

was to be seen

and whereas other children

of the Reagan era not yet grasping this

disease killing off their kind meant *they*

were that kind may have chosen between

flipping through laminated oversized

menus juke

boxes

and the artificial intelligence of micro-pipetting
scrunched-up straw wrappers into *Lumbricidae*

I chose something simpler as
simple as I could imagine

clutching my glass of Pepsi
and in all that revenant dread

my hand went   up
that cylinder

                                                                    and down

sweating the
night's heat   and I

                                                    (disastrous)
didn't under-
stand why

they were
laughing
                                                              up
why what I was
doing was funny
                                                    and

down

                              and

grinning the rictus of
an aspirational bravery as the disquiet of

not understanding dovetailed
with the judgment

swaddled in the Loch Ness mist
of their own seeming amusement,

I said,
        what?
                It feels
        good!
And

they just sat
and laughed.

FORDHAM CASTLE

Like the edge of a road where road meets night where
moon fills the roots of pines with a polar moss where
we lean over shapes you draw with the tip of your cane
like the edge of the road were a cave like this were the
regard or respect we showed for a hunt a matrimony or
soldier the burial of an elder or a mother the drawing
wouldn't say if it was your marriage or someone else's
marriage your burial or my burial the weather we
deprecated or what we besought as though in the hush
between drawing and us it wasn't clear what was falling
out of or into what we remembered what we tried to
tell ourselves we understand if these were being left to
or for ourselves or an ancestor or someone's children
even as sometimes I grieved I had no children through
which nocturnal interval something seeps from the
dark like whistling or a breath pouring through us
transfixed as at the lip of inspiration stealing in in
silence in which gradually what is left of us blurs just
opaque enough to catch some last thread of light in the
plaid edges of its quickly receding branching into the
hidden in itself beguiled as by an inner zenith echo or
absence of nervousness we listened to it the ardor of
listening listening in.

THE SACRED FOUNT / HERBARIUM

The house of fiction had
no doors the eye could
see save one that opened
then open sesame a seed
speeding through itself like
roots through soil we found
ourselves kept close counsel
unto sky in the electrine.

THE SACRED FOUNT / OUR BATTERED
BUT SUFFICIENT VESSELS

Abbé Lazzaro Spallanzani blinded his bats by
inserting hot wire through their corneas or pulling the
eyeballs out snipping them away from their muscular
attachments like an oyster in Hodge's paws whereas
Vassalli who witnessed a fireball ten years prior
sear the early morning sky of Turin poured hot wax
over their eyes then allowed it to cool thereby setting
to silence his nay-sayers whereupon Spallanzani
intransigent placed cotton in the sockets from which
the eyeballs had been removed pasting over these a
leather disk and his bats their bats an attic booby-
trapped with string hung with bells bats hanging
from the rafters feeling in their wings all the agony of
Piemonte the fire that blinded them how clearly they
heard it in their wings the clerestory how they heard
the air of Academical interest in the abbey.

THE AMBASSADORS / SERRANO /
LUXEMBOURG GARDENS

Hearts-gone-roaming
truant under poplars

each little red schoolhouse
shot through with gold

like they too once were
empty things shadows of

acacia deepening the lawn
as inklings grown certain

spilling past one's feet
learning from wayward

umbrae to be drama free if
not discrete oleander roses

redder than sealing wax
crept up the nymphaeum

one careful nearly middle-
aged sole at a time still

planted in the folly and
satyrs rose to meet it all

that willing pallor in their
hands loosely speaking

late blooming left over
alone in banks of blue

smitten with the stillness
of psalms pushing some-

one else's psalms out to
sea.

THE AMBASSADORS / MIDWAY
ALONG THE PATHWAY

Your brain is a lunch bucket with an endless supply
of carrots each morning is seedless grapes an oaty

square the carrots in a small waxed bag every once
in a while fear descends like a groundhog sniffing

air this is your impression of a Dreiser character in a
James novel this is time manly and pregnant as a

seahorse and that's you too poster child for poster
children all shoddy job and celibated turquoise blind

folded in a hanging garden smelling vaguely of
clothespins touching things awake as with a wooden

spoon and this is what gets left its lost remains
ricordo souvenir and something something should

you find yourself on the meddling edge of thinking
of returning to the universe we broke to get you

here, here this viaticum gathered in fine gild print
slight elliptic variations through which chrysograph

we learned to kiss.

THE AMBASSADORS / MARCHONS, MARCHONS

They're meeting in a town called Nevers, which because we're in France is pronounced like a Norwegian saying *no way*. They're living on a houseboat called *Virtuous Attachment*. They have fancy omelet dinners on a gratuitous waterbed. After an evening playing Hart Crane, *Virtuous Attachment* is docked by morning like nothing happened but facemasks and Mille Bornes; like Margaret Fuller and a sherbet bowl of cherry tomatoes. We see right through it, bobbing one harbor over on a dinghy called *Impressionable*. In terms of see right through it, the seagulls are laughing again at my pareo. We take turns with opera glasses, strapped into the director's chair like Hemingway hunting mahi. We take turns being Barbara Bel Geddes. Tonight's special is red herring drone with a side of potatoes hum-drum. We're running out of bigger bait. My nacreous nubile New England pallor has achieved the pink of clafoutis while Chad grows further fulvous by the second. When he do the voodoo. When he clambers aboard deck with thyme in his teeth and acolyte seaweed clinging. The skin-shine makes us squint. Not to mention those propitious little swim trunks. It looks like a hibiscus pattern. I knew his legs from way back when. We're going to make viewfinders for the next purported apocalypse. We're going to launch Platonic his and her fireworks to celebrate our three-week anniversary. From this point forward, everything will have been the future perfect tense. In this way, even talking about the future will have sounded deceptively nostalgic, like peering wistfully from the corner of your eyes while gazing dryly in the opposite direction.

THE AMBASSADORS /
ROTHKO CHAPEL

Entirely by chance
chance   looked
like fate it brought
me here from the
vantage of which
even   furthest
flung   pavilions
of   fine-grained
orrery   affection
turned   cardboard
electrical tape and
resin cut in the
shape of saltern
shadows in the
ragged half light
of which how
could I not become
a   translation   of
the   portrait   of
an action painter
conceding frangible
combustive to the
fungible dark.

THE AMBASSADORS /
ROTHKO CHAPEL

My boy blue holds
out these hands
to show the world
we'd broken is
different from the
one we made I am
being eaten alive a
maroon throbbing
to deeper indigo an
arc keeping us from
and in ourselves
a clearing in the
heart of which
as Boscovich or
Mabel Mercer
writes the
possibility of
nerves re-growing
where nerves were
needed.

THE AMBASSADORS /
ROTHKO CHAPEL

I lived between paint
until it led me here
where they were in
love on a river of
resin ox-blood plum
approaching maroon
roughly   blooming
beneath the varnish
the sun a false sun
sacralizing the new
horizon vanished.

THE AMBASSADORS /
ROTHKO CHAPEL

And maybe when he
returns if he returns
to the world as a
chapel without idols
rent through us to
his heart's content
reaching to a wall a
river where chance
holding fate over resin
means I am being
painted again save
for where my un-
Hellenic ankles were
held where I am being
eaten.

FLICKERBRIDGE

Thence to a watch a weakness morning's first
mosquitoes darning where the sky was eaten

jade wet jade trick of jade perspective deeper
jade I recognize you immediately for whom

the book has what grangered value Sweden-
borgian wring-neck spinny wrought iron gate

two feet of side-chapel dust-light and the dusk
through which it passes. He fell into a sadness

then a fast. It lives there still in the corner of a
Corinthian column. Jewel beetle longborer:

cricket in the masthead not wholly crystalline to
each other a quartz contentment unfastens from

itself an aquarelle sharply mirrored in rushing
water who didn't at some point believe you

would be spared by the cannibal some antique
fragment weather folded soft in an inside pocket.

THE WINGS OF THE DOVE /
THE GRAY IMMENSITY

Sophie Calle once paid an investigator to shadow
her. She went to her favorite places in the city and

he followed, which struck her as romantic despite
their never speaking and when, by chance, their

eyes met they would turn, quickly, different
directions. Mostly she was alone and felt his

presence like the premonition of déjà vu or the
other way round; and to know she wasn't entirely

so, or crazy (so she reasoned to herself) or to give
her investigator the experience (romantic or

paranoid or whatever else it intimated) of being
shadowed or maybe more simply (if this was

simpler) to document the way this relation with
someone bound contractually not to know her

was blooming into these other interesting
scenarios (her motives over-determined as the

romance itself), she hired an investigator to
shadow her investigator. The first investigator:

this was the chronic illness a music so close it
seemed to well inside (it does), and the second

investigator: this is the doctor to whose office we
are walking. And this will be love, too, to hold his

photos in our hands.

THE WINGS OF THE DOVE / EQUAL
TO THE GODS HE SEEMS TO ME

The weight of the tongue plank the breath
winnowed to threading the eye of the needle of

the lung my blood asleep in its wet nest: my body
the skim of it boiled over moonshot flinthead

arrows: this was the pain: mural of a mouth full of
limes one round pearl after another in cursive

loops around the neck self-portrait of a girl
formerly of certain means as the mural of grapes

Roman sparrows break their beaks on the glamour
of it all wasn't longing so much as an acute chronic

preparation for longing. And now when I'm with
you the symptoms vanish vision like water held to

glass my body scraped clean scooped and filled
with quiet light insatiable stupid meniscus when I

saw you my fever dropped.

THE WINGS OF THE DOVE /
TABLEAU VIVANT

You who put this knife in my hand hold it you say for verisimilitude and for
verisimilitude hold it close. To my neck you said and if you're devoted as
you say you'll hold it like Abraham his devotion flailing like a bat

bulb   what was
after bulb   near at hand
                                                    to show
if you are devoted anything something
anything

and the knife.   Look at my face what was once
called what and yours maybe more solemn than when we'd met growing
only further as some would say alarmed   as if this were to what we

were being whittled

and perhaps   being this change or
what you hadn't considered   charge in the heart's   literacy
                                becoming the face of someone else—

devotion of a
sudden flailing and perhaps you see the difference in this change in mine:
your verisimilitude a system vis-à-vis my own and

Please you said

        your   wonderful system   in the same way you said
                having put this this knife in

and   my hand to your neck

and please—   perhaps you'll see not un-suddenly you said
                         (my neck)

Realizing the

difference only in so queer a moment as seeing

                         what it wasn't opening onto what it was
                         becoming if not after the fact than on the lam.

THE WINGS OF THE DOVE /
BARDO

Gold ground painting
bobbin   wound   I
will roar you gently
your silk spooling as
any dove like lace
the ruse of stitches
dropped a brilliancy
indiscernible   from
disgraciousness   as
ornament from orno-
mancy meaning *desp-*
erado the rook deter-
mined [*desperado*] to
give itself forgivance
and   the   angels
laughed   carrying
nothing but flooding
light into gold ground
blinding to a point
and   the   brilliancy
spooling itself in.

THE WINGS OF THE DOVE /
BARDO

Small urn of emptiness
I followed the warmth
of alary rustling ink ball
oak a koan's infrequent
boulders and moraines
from what was left of
slip-shod dimity selvage
a glitch in augury where
pines give way to sky's
idle nesting dolls short-
circuiting November a
single cold composite
sheet of what was left of
all the resinous hearts
towed to harbor all of
which (including mine)
went black a temple
in atrament as though
the moon picked out
a pickerel nearing its
own pale speculation
what you thought being
thought from the cold
black green.

THE WINGS OF THE DOVE /
BARDO

Sieve brain lace brain
sweating its pen-
ultimate secret the
sheets were dank with
it I was a princess
and I stank I turned
clutching clutched
I mean clutched I
will roar you soft
as doves down thou
wilt be a mouse I
saw you the both of
you meaning the two
of you together over-
determined as lace
old lace the brilliancy
of the dismantling
angels un-tying the
everywhere from
everywhere flooding
and my face to the
wall I will roar you
down.

THE ABASEMENT OF THE NORTHMORES

Hope is the thing with
feathers, the fist of a house-

hold god held to the blazing sky of Hiroshima
mon amour, my careful ever. Carved out of honey

blue halo of bees: I can't tell this lone-
someness from the one it's replacing, its heft and harrow

like from covert sprung this hawk with a husband in
its cast bronze hands. Missing quiver, the hypotenuse between

us never seemed so calculable as when your body, my urn of ashes,
bobbed out of reach on the swollen Mersey river.

Hendiadys bowed bent like a hatchet who lives it over by living
back: let me tell you about perforation. I am a badly drawn creature

washed up on a littered shore and hope is the
shells each morning small and cool

into which we hermits
retract the startling

need of our
claws.

THE GOLDEN BOWL / PARTIAL
CONCORDANCE

The way a year ago everything took place. That every-
thing's grave for you is what we take for granted. You

forget everything. The truth of everything I say in ex-
change for "everything." Everything she gave up, letting

everything go but her own disposition. Doing everything
herself. His explanation to her of everything: it sounded

on his lips as if it said everything. Under everything, in
the warm rich earth, their rightness, the justification of

everything. Taking everything from her as harmonious.
For taking everything as it is, everything raised to his lips,

everything around him. Everything became coherent.
Everything fallen together, the grace in everything, your

so much greater knowledge of everything. I've done
earnestly everything I could. She brushed away every-

thing, taking everything as everything came. Did we do
everything to avoid it? Was it the meaning of everything

else? "Everything," she went on, "comes back." If you
knew that you know everything. Everything broke up,

broke down gave way, melted and mingled. Everything
and everyone but the prince. He found everything, for

his interpretation, for his convenience, fall easily enough
into place.

THE GOLDEN BOWL / I CHING /
EGG CUP

During the Inquisition Giambattista della Porta wrote messages on eggshells with a mixture of alum and vinegar. Boiling washed away the alum and when the prisoner peeled the shell the treasonous message was revealed there in the egg white. Your love sours the air it's written on like ink from lemons, time yoking the horizon like the beginning or end of a play. Breakfast egg cup, mouths full of krill: from far enough away waiting for the other to breach the fluke registers only as a little mist, pale gray on gray.

THE GOLDEN BOWL / METAPHRASIS

Dogstar unpronounceable salt in the hurt
of the heart's mouth mumbles courage

bitters vinegar for a brain entrusted with
living in the wake of its only decent logarithm

for approximately feeling a stillness akin
to equipoise for feeling patched up enough

approximately encrusted what better place
than the body's own un-breathable hatch-

battening hive for living out what's left of
a garden lost in the ides of the dog days of

summer the queerness of one's early onset
sexual dementia what's withdrawn versus

vanished in the birth of negative space two
silhouetted faces in profile approaching each

other like they've done this thing before on
the verge each instant of finding each other out

of nowhere becoming a vase an urn I mean I
was being learned the terms of being fumed

like a wasp from the sun-dial silver grid iron of
the pear of anguish hyacinth scold to be by

flight and held to it our necks as for some con-
solation concord or yielding what's left of them

for kissing as by an asp our little in the lost
light delicacy of an imagilet imbordured mis-

remembered as ranunculus trestle lion and
trellis upper mullion from which one might

imagine seeing a person such as this in flight
the difference between which and the blighted

wreck of it being one of use all of it everyone
without remainder in the hive its fiction of

stillness drone and stillness whereas nothing
now is useful here I can't emphasize this

enough June July Judas chair and peony for
demonstrating how little I was being made

to do how it felt to be put to use sunlight since
a misnomer for combustible weathering 2 ft

high in sphagnum what the^song spar.-like
next a nest in wet Andromeda under ^sphag-

num^there with something like a pagoda just
out of bloom and 12 feet high C. oxycantha: A

veronica a book its clean/ sharp/useless///
spine falling like the sun as on a helpless thing

takes someone one as in a poem a carrion a
cornfield a swarm to understand vanishing its

procreant exposure and above it washed over a
temple small boats awash in Oceana roses each

morning woke to gold mine gold Aeneas my
aeneas my aeneas woke to gold each morning

woke we woke and mine is missing.

THE GOLDEN BOWL /
FELIX GONZALEZ-TORRES

I'm lying this lean
heart down

patient as a
dirigent arabesque

colorfield of
gentian foil and

foil a thin sheet of
clouds haunting

the verge escape-
ment foil-back

for relieving the
days of what they

contain afloat
from rocks like

watching an
ocean from the

jetty where a
whale is caught

our first lesson in
forgetting time

was also one in
diluvium one lost

meridian at a time
down welling

what we brought
Sargasso to the

sea from sea and
what it brought.

THE GOLDEN BOWL /
FELIX GONZALEZ-TORRES

There was no other
consideration except

I wanted to make
art work that could

disappear that never
existed and it was a

metaphor for when
Ross was dying it

was a metaphor that
I would abandon

this work before
the work abandoned

me I would destroy
it before it destroyed

this was my little
amount of power

from the very beg-
inning it was not

even there I made
something that does

not exist I control
the pain.

THE GOLDEN BOWL /
FELIX GONZALEZ-TORRES

Perfect lovers two identical
battery-powered clocks side by
side losing synch stopping one
ahead of the other my brave
tangent I am charmed by your
courage and almost surprised
by my own like a hand held to
the pulse of your outer valence
Perfect lovers two identical
battery-powered clocks side by
side losing synch stopping one
ahead of the other my brave
tangent I am charmed by your
courage and almost surprised
by my own like a hand held to
the pulse of your outer valence
Perfect lovers two identical
battery-powered clocks side by
side losing synch stopping one
ahead of the other my brave

THE BEAST IN THE JUNGLE /
HANDFAST POINT

Ricordo a snow globe or old Dutch hour-
glass for searching patience in the broken

open violet of his face a cage turned inward
such as it differed from I did or I could from

you can't the disconcertment of being
caught in the spark chamber of one's own

serially atomizing mendaciousness meant
not being able to remember how it felt not

to be in pain nor quite absolving the avidity
of melancholy twice over some lost fulcrum

as at the end of the blade of an oar folding
open the false sea of etymon spinster from

spintry so named for a bracelet worn on the
upper arm of Roman girls queer Roman

senators countrymen: corruption of *sphincter*
clasping not quite touching meaning no one

to dissuade me from my own errant witness
a filament chiseled into the silver lavender

blue of being ambushed in the deep end of
an armillary learning the feel of Damascene

a centrifuge closing in you seemed to be
saying like it could hold such phosphorizing

sea bed spinel shivery as moths as a moth
being held to the touch.

THE BEAST IN THE JUNGLE /
SAMAHDI

Quiet as ferns in a clearing I fell upon
something like gneiss like Herkimer

diamonds the gloriole electron patience
of stained glass sailors running jewel-like

cellular walls through their impressionable
hands lyke-wake and so alive-like you were

safe in a green delirium of lilies some else-
where ducal palace patient as the misplaced

memory of weather buoying hawks borne
down to what I took for appetite didn't mean

such glint-line lacqueary breaks as the one
we're in weren't also appetite curling fern-like

fractal an ink swashing the earth with us still
in it osmosis a thread-bare curtain of flesh we

try not to shudder behind low-tide star-shot
abandum of the y-axis riveting our shroud-

age pairwise beatified in place as to an under-
water sleep marked by a stone an abstract

felspath remote from the interior and so alive-
like.

A Note on the Text

The New York Editions takes its name from *The New York Edition*, Henry James's name for Scribner's twenty-four volume reissue of the lion's share of his prior novels, novellas, and short stories. In addition, the first half of each poem's title marks a moment in that oeuvre's chronology, from early (*The American*, 1876) to late (*The Golden Bowl*, 1904).

At best superficially allusive, the titular apparatus references James's work as a means of both marking and refracting time, setting into vibration a temporality hovering beyond that of the poems themselves, in which the poems might be said to age. The ensuing rhythm atmospherically traces a measure of intimacy between the poems, their Jamesian counterparts, and the diapason of James's affectively rich encounters in *The New York Edition* with his own earlier, writerly selves.

The poems furnish their own context. In the words of Thoreau, "an echo is, to some extent, an original sound," and if James or his fiction names a solution to them, it's less in the manner of gesturing toward some missing body of knowledge by which poetic meaning is completed or revealed than as sustaining medium ministering solvency if not salvation, "drawn down," James writes, "as by a siren's hand, to where, in the dim underworld of fiction, the great glazed tank of art, strange silent subjects float."

Notes on the Poems

PREFACE

Some of the language of the first section is indebted to that of John Clare, for instance:

> And moody crows beside the road forbear
> To fly, tho' pelted by the passing swain;
> Thus day seems turn'd to night, and tries to wake in vain. ("November")

"The Day is Thine" is the motto of a sun dial on the south-face tower of Saint Guthlac's Church, Market Deeping, Lincolnshire.

In 1794, Lazzaro Spallanzani, an Italian Catholic priest and physiologist, conducted a series of experiments in which he maimed bats by destroying their senses one by one: blinding them, blocking their ears or cutting them off, eliminating their sense of smell, and removing their tongues. His uncanny findings led Spallanzani to postulate a sixth sense, what would eventually come to be known as echolocation.

RODERICK HUDSON / CALLERY PEAR

Informed by the work of James Bidgood, the Maxfield Parrish of gay pornography (baby-oiled Pontormo meets the meretricious aesthetics of Jack Spicer's *Billy the Kid*).

RODERICK HUDSON / MUSE RAGA, F292

With thanks to Michael Harrison for his raga lesson, some summers back among the gold velvet of West House's sitting room.

THE PORTRAIT OF A LADY / MADAME X

"It is as if, in the midst of the figurative and probabilistic givens, a *catastrophe* overcame the canvas." (Gilles Deleuze, *Francis Bacon: The Logic of Sensation*, 82).

THE PORTRAIT OF A LADY / VIGIL

The final clause is adapted from the seventh remove of *The Sovereignty and Goodness of God: Being a Narrative of the Captivity and Restoration of Mrs. Mary Rowlandson* (1682). For CN.

THE PORTRAIT OF A LADY / ILLUMINATED MANUSCRIPT

Informed by Sir Wyke Bayliss's *Seven Angels of the Renascence* (1905). For BB, with gratitude.

THE TURN OF THE SCREW / THAT CALM WE DOOR

Adapted in part from Mike Nichols and Elaine May, "Sonata for Piano and Celeste," for FR & WR. "These postural poles . . ." adapted from Gilles Deleuze, *Cinema 2: The Time-Image*.

THE PRINCESS CASAMASSIMA / FIGURATIVE VERSIONS OF EXCLUSION

Adapted from Michel Henry's *The Essence of Manifestation* and Thomas Traherne's *Meditations*. For AG.

THE SPOILS OF POYNTON / THE SHIMMER OF WROUGHT SUBSTANCES

Adapted from the "secret diaries" of William Byrd of Westover (1674–1744).

WHAT MAISIE KNEW / IN LOCO PARENTIS

Adapted from William Jasper Spillman's *A Theory of Gravitation and Related Phenomena* (1915).

FORDHAM CASTLE

For SS.

THE AMBASSADORS / SERRANO / LUXEMBOURG GARDENS

The title refers to Andres Serrano, American photographer and artist best known for his "Piss Christ" (1987), a photo of a crucifix submerged in the artist's urine.

"Wayward Umbrae" adapted from John Ruskin, "Of Turnerian Mystery."

THE AMBASSADORS / MIDWAY ALONG THE PATHWAY

Title borrowed from Ruth Draper's translation of Dante, from "The Italian Lesson."

FLICKERBRIDGE

For DT, with gratitude.

THE GOLDEN BOWL / I CHING / EGG CUP

For AMH.

THE GOLDEN BOWL / METAPHRASIS

Text adapted in part from the journals of Henry David Thoreau (May 13, 1855–January 3, 1856).

THE GOLDEN BOWL / FELIX GONZALES-TORRES

Text adapted from an *ArtPress* interview of FGT conducted by Robert Storr (1995).

THE BEAST IN THE JUNGLE / SAMAHDI

For EC.

Acknowledgments

I'm grateful to the editors and publishers of the following journals and websites for publishing earlier versions of some of these poems: The Academy of American Poets "Poem-a-Day" Series, *At Length, Fence, Mississippi Review, The Paris Review, PEN Poetry* series, and *Tupelo Quarterly.*

This book wouldn't exist without the alchemizing time and space of Yaddo. My amaranthine thanks to Elaina Richardson and Candace Wait for so many vitalizing summers.

For buoying friendship, vision, and example, my thanks to Margot Backus, Sally Ball, Lauren Berlant, Brian Blanchfield, Tyler Bradway, Kristen Case, Cassandra Cleghorn, Lucy Corin, Colin Dayan (and Stella), Amber Dermont, Alex Dimitrov, Sarah Ehlers, Laurel Farrin, Elisabeth Frost, Jamie Gabbarelli, Andrew Gorin, Peter Gizzi, Louise Glück, Rachel Hadas, Trish Harnetieux, Niki Herd, Mary Hickman, Kevin Holden, Janet Holmes, Anna Maria Hong, Beena Kamlani, Wendy Lee, Thomas Loebel, Jacki Lyden, Fiona Maazel, Airea D. Matthews, Missy Mazzoli, Mark McCray, William McDugald, Maryse Meijer, Lisa L. Moore, Rick Moody, Richard Morrison, Fred Moten, Maggie Nelson, Lisa Olstein, Nancy K. Pearson, Daniel Poppick, Tim Roberts, Brian Rogers, Brian Teare, Roberto Tejeda, Daniel Tiffany, John Emil Vincent, Dara Wier, Elizabeth Willis.

And for Lynn Callahan, most of all.

poets out loud *Prize Winners*

Gary Keenan

Rotary Devotion

Michael D. Snediker

The New York Editions

Gregory Mahrer

A Provisional Map of the Lost Continent

Nancy K. Pearson

The Whole by Contemplation of a Single Bone

Daneen Wardrop

Cyclorama

Terrence Chiusano

On Generation & Corruption

Sara Michas-Martin

Gray Matter

Peter Streckfus

Errings

Amy Sara Carroll

Fannie + Freddie: The Sentimentality of Post–9/11 Pornography

Nicolas Hundley

The Revolver in the Hive

Julie Choffel

The Hello Delay

Michelle Naka Pierce

Continuous Frieze Bordering Red

Leslie C. Chang

Things That No Longer Delight Me

Amy Catanzano

Multiversal

Darcie Dennigan

Corinna A-Maying the Apocalypse

Karin Gottshall

Crocus

Jean Gallagher

This Minute

Lee Robinson
Hearsay

Janet Kaplan
The Glazier's Country

Robert Thomas
Door to Door

Julie Sheehan
Thaw

Jennifer Clarvoe
Invisible Tender

Printed and bound by CPI Group (UK) Ltd, Croydon, CR0 4YY

13/04/2025

14656495-0001